Beautiful Stream
Called Life

Beautiful Stream Called Life

a devotional

MARK A. TURNIPSEED

ISBN: 978-1-7360219-3-4 (paperback)
Library of Congress Control Number: 2022914890

Published by Mark A. Turnipseed Research and Developments, LLC

Cover: Mark A. Turnipseed & Mykhailo Uvarov
Interior Design: Sun Editing & Book Design (suneditwrite.com)

Printed and bound in the USA.

The author of this book does not dispense medical advice or prescribe the use of any technique as a form of treatment for physical, emotional, or medical problems without the advice of a physician, either directly or indirectly. The intent of the author is only to offer information of a general nature based on his own experience. In the event you use any of the information in this book for yourself, the author and the publisher assume no responsibility for your actions.

DEDICATION

As a kid my parents introduced me to Proverbs in the Bible and made me read it every day and I hated it. It's the type of sayings found in Proverbs that help me most as an adult. By teaching me to break life into small, digestible, and transferrable chucks of knowledge I've been able to rise out of all sorts of challenges and to manage, cherish, and to be a good steward of the good times and blessings. Thanks Mom and Dad.

To my coaches, family, and friends who have helped me see through the haze and jump into my beautiful stream called life.

INTRODUCTION

L ife doesn't have to be a never-ending fight and a struggle for control. In fact, the most powerful force in nature is water and it attempts to control nothing. All it does is fall into place. Over and over it just falls into place. When it falls into place it brings with it great purpose, sheer force, and it's always consistent. Where it was dry it becomes wet, where it was thirsty it quenches. Every time.

Our life is not much different than a stream. Some of them have great dams and beautiful lakes emerge. But most of the streams on this planet don't become big lakes. Most of them are simple, untouched, unnoticed, and yet they bring with them just as much life and force on this planet as the ones transformed into lakes.

Contrary to how it may appear, you don't have to control and force your life in certain ways to make it look like another big lake. Your beauty and your wealth-providing, life-giving force is already there. All you must do is learn to tap into this beautiful stream we call life and allow it to fall into place.

The words on the following pages are words that helped me to tap into the beautiful stream of life and if you apply them to your life then they may help you get there, too.

Freedom is being here,
now, and not letting
your past or future
rob you of this moment.

Become centered,
not the center.

Challenge anxiety
with gratitude.

The cloak of shame
casts a shadow telling me
I'm alone when I'm not.
Acceptance brings me
out of that shadow.

Integrity is just doing the right thing even when no one is watching. But it has the power to change everything in your life.

Take a leap
because sitting back
won't get you anywhere.

Self-acceptance is love
and everyone everywhere
deserves love.

If action is the inverse of discomfort, then find ways to challenge your comfort level so that you can activate action and rise to a new life.

Grace frees us from
needing to prove our
worth. Give it so others can
be themselves, accept it
so you can actualize your
potential.

Consistency and
persistency.

Implement those two
things and build belief in
self, achieve goals, and
attain relationships.
Whatever you dream.

When I have self-doubt
I have to just go through
the motions until I build
belief. Push all the way and
hit each small goal with
integrity.

Small successes build
energy and focus while
decreasing self-doubt!

When I grow tired or
stressed and anxious I can
draw closer to those who love
me and find the strength to
pass through anything.

There is great power
in numbers.

I have a choice today
to live through discipline
or wallow tomorrow
in regret.

Search your heart for
any bit of love, sincerity,
serenity, and peace and
plant it as a seed. Water
it and watch it grow and
consume your world.

Each day is filled
with moments you can
seize the opportunity to
get closer to a dream.

Pull restlessness together
by connecting movement
with the mind.

This is mindfulness.

This is yoga.

Each day is a path
paved with moments of
opportunity to get closer
to a dream.

Practice doesn't necessarily make things easier in life but the motions become a part of your system and a part of your being and through that anything becomes possible.

Watch for bitterness.
The smallest amount
can ruin a great day.

The best medicine for
emotional health is to find
a way help another.

The path to loving
yourself starts with helping
others and the path to
loving others starts with
loving yourself.

Ego tells me I'm alone
and it's me against an evil
world while grace shows me
I'm part of a greater whole
that makes up a good world.

Today I choose to walk
with grace, not ego.

Learning to sit with pain
helps us grow more respect
for pleasure.

Use fear only to help you
prepare so when the time
comes you can conquer.

Search less
for feelings of motivation
for those feelings undulate
like the tide. Rather, seek
more for YOUR WHY
to drive you towards
greatness.

You are not your feelings.

Discomfort can create mental toughness. It's okay to be uncomfortable. Discomfort is a perfect time to explore and exploit weakness while gaining insight into how to grow stronger.

Sometimes to simply show
up is the best we can do

and that
really
is
okay.

Let go

Let God.

Enjoy yourself
and find light heartedness,
your bliss.

With integrity
there is no fear and no
reason to hold back.

Perseverance is sticking to
what matters most
despite feeling weak,
melancholy, or isolated.

Where your focus is
dictates where
your path leads.

When it gets hard
concentrate on how I
hold myself and not on
the finish line or what I'm
trying to accomplish.

Sometimes all I can do
is stand up straight and
meditate on the form of the
here and now and if I keep
doing that over and over
day in day out ...
I'll get there.

It's okay, no, it's good
for you to laugh at yourself
from time to time.

Sharing with others
how life is hard and difficult
is very important.

I'm worth the breath.
I'm worth the mornings.
I'm worth the hard work.

Taking it slow is one of
the hardest disciplines.

The words "I can" and "I can't"
come from the same mind
out of the same lips
and I control both.

It's okay to not feel okay.
It's okay to be afraid. It's
okay to be sad, mad, manic.
It's also okay to utilize
these emotions to guide
your next move.

The greatest of victories
and the hugest successes
are surmounted one day
at a time.

If it seems insurmountable,
think smaller because right
now it's just for today.

The world needs YOU.

The world doesn't need
the person people want
you to be.

The world needs
the person you ARE.

If you are desperate to
find the beauty within,
you will begin seeing the
beauty without. You will see
that you are not alone and
will join all that which is
beautiful.

Find small success in your
day and begin labeling
yourself for what you are:
A Winner.

Align your breathing
with your heart, first thing,
before you rise from bed.

Being uncomfortable in a
controllable environment
(fitness, cold showers, fasting)
helps us to regain power
and reduce anxiety
in the uncontrollable
uncomfortable situations.

FEAR

Face
Everything
And
Rise

OR

Fear
Everything
And
Run

Confidence is not
fearlessness, it's
the willingness
to stand up to fear.

Approach everything
and everyone with more
curiosity than opinion.

When in an argument
ask yourself if you'd rather
be happy, or right.

Giving a name
to your struggles can
help you see them
for what they are.

You don't become
your thoughts or feelings,
but you do become known
by your actions.

Emotions oscillate,
gratitude grounds!

Let life be like sushi
and take the whole bite.

Sometimes it's easier
to find that which is
controllable by naming,
counting, looking and
accepting that which isn't.

Learning to control the
breath is mastery in life
for even if life spirals
unbridled, breath can
remain tight in reign.

We can build on our
gifts and learn from our
mistakes when we measure
decisions with the balance
of gratitude and reflection.

Never underestimate
the strength and growth
that occurs when you
remain neutral during an
opinionated argument.

It's better to struggle
through a challenge, or
even fail at a challenge,
than it is to live a lie.

Break each day up into small tasks and do each task well but before you task anything out start by making the bed.

Has negativity climbed
into the garden of my life?
Make a gratitude list every
day until the good pushes
out the bad.

The person I dream
of becoming
is waiting for me to
let go of the person
I'm attached to being.

Understanding that others,
too, are lonely and scared
and have the basic desire
to be safe and respected
and heard is very essential
to finding peace and calm
when humanity seems crazy.

It's also the starting point
of compassion.

Instead of fearing
the unknowns in my life
I'll take time to explore them
and to become educated.

Finding small goals in
a big journey, like fitness or
work, can bring the joy
out of the labor.

If you are consistent
with thought and action,
you can rise above any
thought or bad habit
that is holding you back.

Remember, there is always
a great and bright light
laying just beyond any
cloud, no matter how dark.

I'll use the little things
to prove to myself that I'm a
success and as I add them up
others will see it, too.

Fight discontentment
with self-compassion.

(Compassion comes from a Latin
word that means to suffer with.
When we can embrace our
suffering the longing and want
that's fueling discontentment
leaves us.)

Delayed satisfaction
will lead to prolonged
gratification while instant
gratification leads to low
self-satisfaction.

Rather than running from
your fears only for them
to take you over after you
become exhausted, try
running with your fears so
that when the time comes
you can beat them at the
finish line.

There is no sense in
dwelling on how much I
don't like what I've become
when I don't have to stay.

The greatest time to learn
about myself is when things
don't go as planned.

Unhappiness is solved
in three steps:

1. Acceptance

2. Compassion

3. Giving Back

Think more about the
things you want to embody
and entertain not
the things you don't.

How much more beautiful
is a garden with
more than just roses?

Let kindness and unity
decide if a conversation
is worth engaging in.

Be most kind to those
with whom you disagree.

"If I don't like someone
it's because I haven't spent
enough time with them."

—Abraham Lincoln

In all things
decide to blossom
rather than protect.

Vulnerability leads
to great growth.

Be wary of those things
that in their absence
you collapse.

Rid yourself of toxic
attachment or always out of
reach serenity will be.

Confidence is
a fleeting feeling

while

Faith is
a state of being.

Optimism is only the
illusion of hope.

Where optimism fails,
hope prevails.

Faith that good will come
is much easier to maintain
when I know I'm living
a life built with integrity
and honesty.

How much better is a
waterfall than a stagnant
pool?

Be okay with giving into
the flow and falling.

When a wish becomes a
want we shift from living
in the great world of
possibility to drowning in
the pain of expectation and
entitlement.

Keep dreaming but
avoid wanting.

Spending time naked
can improve self-esteem.

Choosing daily self-improvement can be as simple as staying away from things that harm you. This will put you on a path towards awakening even if you don't believe it.

Bravery is just accepting
that you may not be
comfortable, but you are
going to do it anyway.
Practice it with the small
things: fitness, socializing,
cooking.

Treat relationships like
a rose bush. Tend to them
and allow them to flourish.

Spend more time
overcoming negativity
within than arguing
with others.

Keep it simple
and just
Show Up.

When life gets hard,
confusing, disordered or
overwhelming I like to
find the simple pleasures—
like blowing bubbles
underwater.

If I'm having a hard time
with self-acceptance it's
most likely because I'm
concentrating on my
perceived limitations
and not my potential.

Always be quick to meet
failure with contemplation
so that it doesn't take root
and manifest into identity.

Contemplation will help
you grow stronger from
your failures.

After you contemplate,
leave the past behind.

I'll set my mind on the hard and rewarding path to avoid the easy and destructive one.

A mindful vacation can
happen throughout any day
and restore you as much as
a week-long destination.

There's a reason why we
grow and learn so well
throughout childhood, play.

Don't allow the act of play
to be a thing left behind.

It's possible to rewire the
brain to see challenge
as opportunity.

Acceptance, though
it may seem contrary,
can be the first step
in overcoming an obstacle.

There's no way to know if
you can until you try
and there's no better time
to try than now.

Don't let the time pass you by.

Be your own hero.

If you show up for yourself
you will begin to see that
you are perfect, beautiful
the way you are, and wholly
needed to fill a void that
the world has without you.
You can do this!

With time, good habits
become part of identity
and the question of
where to find motivation
disappears and becomes
irrelevant.

Self-acceptance is the
mortar that binds our brick
when building our tower
from weakness to strength.

The only limitation that
will defeat me today is
my belief and attachment
to my own perceived
limitations.

Integrity should not be
confused with piety.

Integrity is listening to
what's in your heart,
not the conviction of others.

Be true to yourself
because only then will you
reap the rewards of integrity.

Each day you choose to
show up for yourself
you make this world
a better place.

Be unapologetically you,
we need you.

I used to look for differences
to feel unique and I found
loneliness and pity parties.

Now I look for similarities
and I find strength, community,
and victories.

Rise in the morning as if
you're rising to greatness
and take each step as if
you're walking to glory,
because this day is your
chance to leave your legacy.

Gratitude prolongs
endurance by strengthening
our ability to move through
that which we didn't think
we could handle.

In the stillness of the heart
you find the warrior
in a person.

You can act your way into
feeling long before you can
feel your way into action.

Don't wait to feel motivated,
just do it.

Integrity is listening to
the gentle whisper inside
that leads us always on the
path of becoming our
best self.

Listening
is one of the greatest gifts
you can give another.

When it comes down to it the only choice we have is to follow our truth or not. Truth, will ultimately set you free if you continue to follow it.

Dreams come true
by taking each moment,
giving it your best, and
adding them all together.

(O)pinion is about as useful
as ash: it does nothing to
help a good fire burn.

Beauty is only experienced
when present in the
moment.

If I don't feel beautiful,
I need to get grounded.

When I chose to see I wasn't
alone in my struggle, the
world opened and out of
my struggles emerged
my greatest strengths.

I learned early on in my
fight against depression that
if I wasn't walking forward,
I was slipping back.
There was no middle ground,
there is no stagnant point.
It's forward or it got worse.

The loneliness
that drove me to suicide and
addiction was a condition
of my mind that was just
waiting to be reconciled by
reaching out for help.
It worked.

Wishing for dreams is one thing, accepting them when they come is another.

Many of us are already living our dreams today and just need a shift in perspective to see it.

In developing relationships
remember that a shared
genuine interest in
knowledge and experience
is a stronger foundation
than shared opinions,
preferences, and tastes.

Learning and practicing
the art of forgiveness with
the small things in daily life
(like someone forgetting to
put a blinker on) can help
us to eventually tackle and
overcome those big lifelong
things that rip our
heart apart.

Together we can rise from anything we've broken, alone we will cave in on everything we've built.

Your best self is always
there, gently nudging like
a cool breeze on a calm lake,
guiding you towards
your truth.

If you listen and adjust
your sail, you'll find you
already have available what
you think you're missing.

Using fear
as an opportunity to make
changes, adjustments, and
to learn about ourselves
is okay, but when we let it
drive us, we become
a slave to it.

Integrity is essentially
consistency and harmony
with morals and action
and character.

Identifying grace in your
heart allows you to learn to
appreciate more the time
between dreams so that
the real wild dreams have
room to come true.

View blessings
as responsibility,
not entitlement, and
watch the universe
keep giving.

The world is waiting for
you and needs you and
loves you, but only when
you come dressed as you.

Gratitude is an inner
choice not dependent on
exterior circumstance.

Find gratitude inside first
and the rest will follow.

Realizing you aren't
alone is the first step to
understanding just how
essential you truly are.

Division only really happens
when we don't look hard enough
for similarities and likeness.

It's never too late to step
back, restart, reimagine,
and reinvent. It's only my
attachment and pride
that say otherwise.

Fear, resentment, and
pride were the only things
keeping me from prayer and
a relationship with God, but
fear, resentment, and pride
no longer rule my life.

Prayer does.

Today is a gift for everyone
and each person should be
treated as if they deserve
this most wonderful gift.

Be kind, breathe life.

The spirit rests easy
when the body and mind
are clear of the clutter
from the what if's,
the should have's,
and the wish I had's.

Integrity can help this.

Guilt is replaced by
joy when acceptance,
authenticity and truth
take the rein within.

When you can't feel
the wind it's generally
because it's assisting you
by blowing from behind.

There is power in what
you call yourself. Stand
today and call yourself
what you are:

Beautiful.

There are those who seek to make their own world a better place and others who seek to make *THE* world a better place.

Integrity involves ditching
expectations and resolving
internal homeostasis by
recovering your bliss.

You have the super-power
of being you today
and that's the best thing
the world could have.

The seemingly still and small voice within you speaking greatness and kindness into others is the most powerful and loud tool on this earth.

It can move mountains.

Your past is only a
representation of what was
and until you let go it will
keep repeating itself.

The good news is
you can start changing
direction any day.

Welcome discomfort as a chance to connect with your limits, gain mastery of your breath, and filter your negative chatter.

Uncertainty is just an
opportunity to test faith
and continue to place one
foot in front of the next.
It comes to all of us at times.
No need to fear it.

Only when we scrub
our soul of indifference
can we wear the badge
of compassion and rise
together in pride.

Learning to accept oneself
can change your world ...
learning to accept others
can change THE world.

ABOUT THE AUTHOR
MARK ADAMS TURNIPSEED

Author, motivational speaker, coach, LGBTQ addiction recovery advocate, practicing wellness expert, and entrepreneur, Mark A. Turnipseed is the author of "Following Your Bliss into the Beautiful Stream Called Life" and the Amazon bestseller, "My Suicide Race: winning over the trauma of addiction, recovery and coming out.

Focused on good health, self-acceptance, and authenticity, Mark shares how you can tap into your best self through the daily practice of compassion and self-acceptance. Sharing his own recovery story to inspire and motivate others, Mark discusses the health-focused tools he has used to overcome challenges and embrace aspects of yourself that limit you from your potential. As a keynote speaker and workshop leader, Mark speaks about unlocking your potential in the physical, emotional, and spiritual realm. Mark has also found a novel approach to helping people with mental health by using skin care and mindfulness to accept self, accept others and embody beauty in his work with his inclusive focused wellness, lifestyle and skincare line called Halo 42.

For booking and additional information visit:

www.markaturnipseed.com

Twitter: @markaturnipseed

Instagram: @markaturnipseed

Facebook: @markaturnipseed

CPSIA information can be obtained
at www.ICGtesting.com
Printed in the USA
LVHW012139121022
730573LV00003B/197